WITCH DOCTRINE

AKRON SERIES IN POETRY

AKRON SERIES IN POETRY
Mary Biddinger, Editor

Annah Browning, *Witch Doctrine*
Emily Corwin, *Sensorium*
Kimberly Quiogue Andrews, *A Brief History of Fruit*
Joshua Harmon, *The Soft Path*
Oliver de la Paz, *The Boy in the Labyrinth*
Krystal Languell, *Quite Apart*
Brittany Cavallaro, *Unhistorical*
Tyler Mills, *Hawk Parable*
Caryl Pagel, *Twice Told*
Emily Rosko, *Weather Inventions*
Emilia Phillips, *Empty Clip*
Anne Barngrover, *Brazen Creature*
Matthew Guenette, *Vasectomania*
Sandra Simonds, *Further Problems with Pleasure*
Leslie Harrison, *The Book of Endings*
Emilia Phillips, *Groundspeed*
Philip Metres, *Pictures at an Exhibition: A Petersburg Album*
Jennifer Moore, *The Veronica Maneuver*
Brittany Cavallaro, *Girl-King*
Oliver de la Paz, *Post Subject: A Fable*
John Repp, *Fat Jersey Blues*
Emilia Phillips, *Signaletics*
Seth Abramson, *Thievery*
Steve Kistulentz, *Little Black Daydream*
Jason Bredle, *Carnival*
Emily Rosko, *Prop Rockery*
Alison Pelegrin, *Hurricane Party*
Matthew Guenette, *American Busboy*
Joshua Harmon, *Le Spleen de Poughkeepsie*

Titles published since 2011.
For a complete listing of titles published in the series,
go to www.uakron.edu/uapress/poetry.

WITCH
DOCTRINE

ANNAH BROWNING

 The University of Akron Press
Akron, Ohio

Copyright © 2020 by The University of Akron Press
All rights reserved • First Edition 2020 • Manufactured in the United States of America.
All inquiries and permission requests should be addressed to the publisher,
The University of Akron Press, Akron, Ohio 44325-1703.

ISBN: 978-1-629221-64-9 (paper)
ISBN: 978-1-629221-65-6 (ePDF)
ISBN: 978-1-629221-66-3 (ePub)

LIBRARY OF CONGRESS CATALOGING-IN-PUBLICATION DATA
Names: Browning, Annah, author.
Title: Witch doctrine / Annah Browning.
Description: First edition. | Akron, Ohio : The University of Akron Press, 2020. |
    Series: Akron series in poetry
Identifiers: LCCN 2019046244 (print) | LCCN 2019046245 (ebook) | ISBN
    9781629221649 (paperback ; alk. paper) | ISBN 9781629221656 (pdf) | ISBN
    9781629221663 (epub)
Subjects: LCSH: Witchcraft—Poetry. | LCGFT: Poetry.
Classification: LCC PS3602.R7374 W58 2020 (print) | LCC PS3602.R7374 (ebook) |
    DDC 811/.6—dc23
LC record available at https://lccn.loc.gov/2019046244
LC ebook record available at https://lccn.loc.gov/2019046245

∞The paper used in this publication meets the minimum requirements of ANSI/NISO
z39.48–1992 (Permanence of Paper).

Cover image: *Blue Meadow* by Kelly Louise Judd. Cover design by Amy Freels.

Witch Doctrine was designed and typeset in Minion with Futura display by Amy Freels
and printed on sixty-pound natural and bound by Bookmasters of Ashland, Ohio.

**Affordable
Learning Initiative**
THE UNIVERSITY OF AKRON

Produced in conjunction with the University
of Akron Affordable Learning Initiative.
More information is available at
www.uakron.edu/affordablelearning/.

Contents

III.

I.

Spell for a Lover

My addle-winged darling.
Stir-fried flyer. Come on

down, and grease this
pan. Fat of your body

glowing in the sun. Amber
jelly and my hair sucked

into your mouth,
in the wind. Trace the sign

of the cross on the back
of my hand again, begging it

to *find you, find you*. A lantern
is just a piece of contained fire,

something that wants to eat
you alive. Follow me, your marsh

-light, your baby dying
in the crowning, the gold-headed

not-ever-servant undressing
in the field, stepping out of her

clothes into the night. Toad-bride
pissing on your hand.

Witch in Winter

Come, let the ice file in. Come,
      let the spindly roosters

scratch their homes in me.
      I am always watching.

The shadow of the house—
      it watches, too. Its eaves

are sloping, caring; wooden
      and wise it lowers

its windows, shades drawing
      the light down

to a close. Now, I will have
      to be good. I spell out

a message with berries; I leave
      you some cursive

in thorns. Without the light,
      it is something I have

to believe—that the snow is
      adding to me,

that the animals do not climb
      all over, their feet

lifting up these words.

Witch as Healer

I like to roost
in the minds of others,

like a blackbird
in the rafters of

a church—heaven,
hell, the fiend all

below. And the lux
of so many heads—

their hair, black, blonde
and white, spun whorling

from the crown, light
of day and light

of night. I peer
into their ears and nuzzle

the small bones
of their sadness. I grow

amusing, sleeping
at their height. *You've*

got a devil on your
shoulder, one'll say,

and might be right.
I give each of my visitors

a name—they're never told
it, but they respond to

it. Their hearts yield
like flesh to a knife—

their chins fall on
their lovers' hands so slightly.

When they sleep, I love
them best—I stir,

slur their dreams
with a beak, a talon,

a warbled song—
a cry, and then some rest.

Witch's Homunculus

I am not a person.
I am a collection of branches.

A stand of trees
at a distance, named

for what they do.
You can call me

with the cup of your hand
over your mouth,

a finger rubbed behind
the ear, a whistle that's low

first, then eerie.
When a sound

goes old you can feel it.
The age stretches it out.

It rusts in air. My hair
gets rusty, knots at the scalp

like cumulous clouds.
I would share

this afternoon with you,
but I ate it all. I gnawed

it down to a last corner
of light in the bedroom,

like the rind of a cheese,
the skin of a fowl—at first

found delicious, then,
not enough—with grease

on the blankets
I leave this here,

the shape of my lips, face—
a kiss for mama.

Witch to Familiar

Sorry eyes. Almost bruises.
        Let me clean your glasses

for you, evil pet of mine. I'll
        take you, tweedly, into

my lap. Wrapped up in your
        own sleeves. I had to put

a part of my brain to sleep
        to do this. I had to use

a long needle and some thread.
        The forest is clamoring

for these eyes. The firs all waving
        around, looking

for somebody with something
        to say. You don't; you just

look around. Burrow south
        for safety. Yes, that's

my lap; I'm not a kneeler.
        I'm not some handkerchief

for you to cry in, though of course
        you're crying now. Pet, pet,

pet. How could I leave you frozen
        when there are so few

others? How could I turn
        the whistle away, when the wind

opened up my door?

Witch Doctrine: On Giving Prescriptions

All your words must bend
towards hope. Most birds

are no messengers.
Read their guts, then

fall asleep. Dream
avalanche, dream crowding

sternums, claws, the opal
of a replaceable eye.

Its glass shines clearly,
and in your stomach

the harvested hours
turn over, and go silent,

stillborn as magic. Just
tell your visitors, *A poultice*

for your privates, Ma'am—
this drink, if shaken, works

for fever, the night-destroyer—
say, *Take this and wake*

in the morning more solid,
and they will, stand wet

and clean as a calf surviving
calving, one who tries out

the ground. The star on its
forehead growing out. Blazing.

Witch Questions the So-Called Higher Power

The last time I conversed
with the Great Sentience,

I asked, *What the hell
are you doing?* and

He gestured at some
cobwebs, books that

needed straightening,
spiders announcing

their localities everywhere
by wrapping up their dead,

that is to say, meals
and recently mated ones

"For later," as we often say,
making several assumptions

at once, particularly latter-ness
and how nice an intention

can be, when more often,
as Great Fathers have

frequently done, He's
going to just walk out

and leave this horrible
mess behind, things

like cow mutilations,
the removed lips

and anus, the perfect
excision-work of maggots,

who are really only
children, still growing

up, eating all the soft
things so they can grow,

melt into metallic, bullet
-like wings, to visit other

bodies, landscapes
which, if they were human

they would think they
discovered first, as if

the wet birth caul
covering the face had never

happened, and no one
had ever said, *Now here's*

a lucky one.

Witch Lullaby

What if my sideways smile
slipped down a little,

did not behave? Darling
Sister, love me, do you

not, unbraiding your hair
into waves? Our house rocks

like a ship at sea; our house
hums in the night. Planets

coast by like peculiar eyes,
pinpricks in the glass

of the window. Sing, Oh Consonant,
Oh Vowel. Oh Consonant again.

Speech between your lips
lumpy as soup, burning like gin.

Breathe on me, so softly.
Bring me nightmares again.

Witch Dreams of Happiness

In continual guidance towards
the light, I walked forever,

my trepanned skull whistling
in the wind, an extra coal eye

from which I was seeing all color.
And the shadows on the inside

of my eggshell face had never
made such pleasing shapes,

birds and trees and mammals
who expressed no interest

in eating me, only licking
my ears and reminding me

how precious it is to hear
breathing on your neck

when you have allowed it,
when you have asked

for it, said, *Please come
here, I would like to feel*

*your fur and pulse,
and shiver, Sugar—*

Witch as La Belle Dame

Don't forget to love me.
I require it, my milky eyes
require it, and furthermore

I won't let you get farther
than the sycamore tree.
Lie down and be a map

for dew and frost, my finger-
nail traced paths, for
the changelings I will

beget and leave forgot.
Turn your head a little.
Tilt, planetary—this ear

gets a vernal equinox,
sun-crossed, and every
rabbit I send for you

to eat will only be
a little rabid, a little
lean—oh isn't this

the privacy you wanted?
This night is the good
bath. I'm going to lick you
        clean—*sans merci*—

Witch Doctrine: Comfort

When your heart feels
evil, don't make it

lie to you. Place your
neck on the cold table

and feel warm wind
rising behind you,

tossing the trees
like a young woman

waking up to thrash
her hair with a brush.

Don't be afraid
of the wasp prickling

its slim legs on
the hair of your arm.

Listen. Every day
a match is struck

and rubbed out
on the skyline.

Final Witch Doctrine

The old ones say to draw
       your broom across

the step, then pull the latch.
       On the snow's arrival,

witch doctrine says, you bring
       the dogs in. No howlers

left alone. The gray muzzled
       and the slow-cancered, their

heavy bellies wander home, and
       the skinny ones, too, those

you feed dark chicken blood—
       a canine wine. But remember,

daughter: there are nights you'll have
       to walk out alone. Know

there's nothing so bad about
       a cold wind reaching

through your shirt to your
       chest, the strong

contraction of your stomach—
       it says, *Keep walking.* A long

winter is ahead, and you'll study it
       like a lover. You'll learn

its white sides and its gray
        sides; you'll learn branches' pop

and crack, their glassy reflections.
        And when one whips

your cheek like a hot blade, you'll
        thank it. You'll take

another branch for the fire,
        and you will make it.

Witch Passing the Graveyard

All of the little dead ones sing, *Ah-ah-ah*—
and the bigger ones say nothing
behind flat faces. They tag behind

me in the trees, cast a perfumed light,
too sweet, too cold, chilled floral
hum burrowing in the back

of my throat. I can turn it
in my mouth like a loose tooth
I am so afraid of swallowing—

this sharpness I was not prepared for—
carrying a basket of herbs and late
summer clothes. If only laying a man

down was as easy as folding his shirts—
crossing arms and shoulders, then
bending it all back—I like to kiss

the place where his neck
was before, and leave my breath
there, a little bloom of heat.

Southern Witch Doctrine on the Resurrection

If I never resurrect,
I shall not be forlorn.

I'll get eat up by the red
slick clay that's colored

my hair since before
I was born. If I am never

born again, I hope the dirt
shall fill my head

with quartz-rock arrowheads
buried white as the stars

I rarely looked at. I rest
in hope that I will never rest

in hope. I've torn out too much
muscle with my teeth,

too much blood's run down
my legs, and I've laughed too

high and hard—*I'd rather
die,* I said once, and I meant it.

I'd rather not respond
to a single knock at my door

that asks if I'd like to go
someplace clear

and bright—my face is humid,
my hair a root storm rising

in the flood, and if they say
skulls are always smiling

mine's just saying, *Hey there,*
hello, hi, look at my teeth

carving out my wet black cake
of leaves, my slice of old dark night.

Witch after Heartbreak

I have decided not to stop
loving. Mostly because the fingers
will not grow back anyway.

With the middle two half-bitten,
I look like I'm always making

the I-love-you sign, or gesturing
to the distance on a map
that is of course muddy, but

I'm confident, because I've made
this journey before. Over hills black

and flat as paper, my body sliding
between them like a letter
in a dark envelope, arriving

into another such hollow,
holler, what I have to do
just to forget being found.

Witch Kills the Familiar

This morning I killed the familiar.
He had asked me to several times, usually

in the mornings, when he straightened
out his broken back to walk, crackling

like the fire I breathed into his lips.
Long, long ago. I excavated him dank

-furred from the well, scryed his eyes,
lifted him up from my reflection. He was

screaming. Only natural things have
patience. A stone will sit and be wept

over for a thousand years. Dead trees
will be planked, wet and swept,

by a least a dozen daughters left
behind. But familiars—they won't

be coaxed. They sing to me
in their gravel voices, and beg

to die. I took him out to the apple trees,
and told him, *What you will*. He unrolled

out of his skin like a flower in a fire,
his hide a black erupting lily,

smelling not like food, but like work.
I will have to make another man.

II.

Spell for a Daughter

Have a daughter, call her Asylum.
Have a daughter, call her Better
Late. Have a daughter.

Call her Christian. Call her
Beget-by-Fate. She is the called-
back, she is a dead horse,

she is the one arisen, and she
is lovely. She holds your hand
until it purples. She twists

her hair until it's snakes.
She is born, she is born,
she is born. She whispers

to you—always late and
never better. Always in
the lake and shining. She is

your daughter, you beget
her. Her teeth are even
and small, and they wait.

Dream of Flat Hills

I went a long time into the disquiet.
          I called my names out. Skies

were clearing. Stones like jawbones
          covered the field. There

was a long crease—the place
          where hills had met. I said,

I'll try and lie down here; I'll try
          and get some sleep. Murderers

stood on the edge of the deep
          and were lonely. They waved

all their shovels at me—goodness—
          goodness, I said—it must

be something like this.

To the Salt Gator

Piano key belly, scales like
        calico corn. Your one eye

gone white from salt-blindness,
        river-animal too long

in the sea. I see your smooth
        hooks, your eye-teeth

above water, jaws open
        and shut like a new

book. Your tongue says chicken,
        horse meat, unfortunate

goat, but your neck reads salt
        line, sand, an open boat—

how hard you had to swim
        to figure out a new

darkness there, each waterfowl
        receding, the sun's white

feathers collapsing into the mouth
        of an older god.

Dear Ghost:

I am not good at telling
if you are real. Do me
the favor of existing,

please. Press your face
into the burn of the toast,
or clearly film the bathroom

mirror. I would love
to call you ghost, or house-
mate, or even house—

is that you in the pipes,
whistle-buddy? I don't
know. I drink my coffee

black as hair. When I
come inside, I cradle
the newspaper like a child,

a gray baby full of new
bad words. Did I say it
out loud, this bit about

the eye cancer that burrows
in the rods and cones?
A color-cancer. I think

you like things faded.
I think you love an oatmeal,
a wet sock, the salt line

on a boot. Where the world
licks us, passing by.

Collector of Luck

I am afraid there is
something terrible

wrong with me. I go
about my night things.

My walk makes a sound
like *this, this—this, this—*

footsoles shushing
the floorboards, whispering,

Trust—that the stair will be
there, when I'm able

to cross it. When I can. I look
in on my books like infants—

Oh, you sleep so well, Jericho,
and Deuteronomy, and all

the other names I keep
in books with leaves

and four-leaf clovers—or
almost four-leaf clovers.

Whatever luck is possible
in pressed lettuce, or tulips—

what is too full of rain
to really keep, but not

to love. This penny
I glue to the bottom

of my shoe, keep treading
on—the face of the dead

good man kissing
whatever I cross.

Where to Look for Ghosts

Places you can pin one:
under a backseat; smeared

into a cushion with gum;
a long reflection

in a butter knife; sawdust
from building

an unused piece
of furniture. Dying plants,

mice removed from
a carbine harvester.

Willow trees. In the purses
of old women who live

by lakes. Fertilizer, seeds
scattered on a windowsill;

rain left to dry most
anywhere. Violent thoughts,

syrup left blackening
on the tabletop; ink on the fat

of a palm. Forks with broken
tines, held up like a hand

after a mechanical mishap—
phantom pain.

Widow: Out-of-Body Experience

My persona sits in the room.
Her eye reflects the fire

like a struck match. These
are her hands, shuddering,

her teeth graying with
the afternoon. No one here

is carnivorous now that he
is gone. The plants continue

their silent drinking from roots
I can't see. Mice I imagine,

though they can't talk
the way the wood talks, gloss

squeaking under fingers.
It's the solitary death

of the day. Dishes slide
like a white accordion,

dark stains running down
their centers, a brown bloom

here and then gray ones,
on the plates deeper

down—call it a meal
ghost. God is not looking.

God does not observe
the tiny wing bones,

the film and the original
skin—charred and flattened

like a pressed flower. *Bon
anniversaire*, my charming

man. Your mouth left
behind these unnamed

valleys, these hills
and peaks in bread.

For you I would
give up all my ghosts.

Medium in the Morning

I have been sleeping strangely—
I've been living with

a song, that on and off
vibrates me like a beehive—

head on the floor—I hear
the flood of kazoos, dead people

doing their morning or evening
washing. Whatever

it is down there. I hear
the tinny singing of the spirits

and long for, I don't know
exactly what—a new geranium,

something red, something I can't
take my eyes off of—you know,

how they tell you to balance:
pick one spot to fixate on.

They say I live like Gemini,
the twins, or Rhodes—one leg

in this world, one slung over
into the next. I ride a bad,

bad horse. I'm so tired
of being vital, of herding

the mothers and the widows.
Gaslight murders my stomach.

Like all armies, the dead
march there, gobbling up

my perfume, the weather,
the communion of the saints—

What wafer-thin things
their children are, conceived

in this life, born in the next,
toddling without lungs.

Their insides are black as the cores
of old apples, pistol shine,

my eyes in the kitchen window
washing up, saying, *What art thou*

doing today? Then I wipe
away the tea leaves, and try again.

Personal Cleansings

from The Encyclopedia of 5,000 Spells

Many personal cleansings, particularly
baths, may be performed for oneself. Choose
cleansing assistants wisely. You can't really

sweep yourself. Obtain as many kinds
of citrus fruits as possible. Keep proportions
equal. Eggs are believed to be extremely

absorbent. Take an egg outside, far
from home, and smash it on the ground.
Coconuts also work, but don't forget—

coconuts are harder. Stronger action
needs to be taken. In theory, one should use
fertilized eggs so that the possibility

of blood exists. Undress completely. If you can,
have someone else perform the egg-rubbing
and parsley-slapping parts. This is particularly

refreshing if Florida Water is kept chilled
in the refrigerator. Get into bed and burn
for the next twenty-four hours. Soak

a photograph in saltwater. When seven
waves have passed over you, the cleansing
is over. You will know which photograph to use.

Medium after Producing the Ectoplasm

I pat the ectoplasm on the table
and watch it dry. Wax and cheese-
cloth, the intestine of a sheep,

yellow-white frilly loveliness.
If this is a metaphor, it is for
the oldest aproned frocks, for when

I was a girl who still believed
I would blossom, turn into
my mother: classically

disinterested, diaphanous
as candles. Still, I have not died.
If I pull this substance

from my thighs, the widows think
I have been somewhere, and gasp,
and the knocks in the walls sound

like rabbit ghosts—the pounding
of what wants to remain invisible.
Rain-like—the running patter

of rats above my head when
I'm sleeping, the trickle sound
of their teeth gnawing the headboards.

And I remember feeling the velvet
of another woman's skin
when I was helping her into a bath

before she was married, and when
my hand dropped like a pebble
in the water, it was slick white

and useless, much as a soul is.

Medium after Trances

Every time I come back,
I am a little different.

Every time I get up
from the river of sleep,

I breathe differently,
believe in wings, whine

over stones like a dog
who's been told

she's been bad. Remind
me tomorrow to tell

you what I have done
in a dream—who I killed,

what I left un-cauterized,
what nail shivered

in the light where I left
it for the next approaching

foot, rust and rubble,
the gray crow shuddering

inside an apple tree—
at least, I believe it was there—

breathing with the tree,
filling with bees, wasps—

the stings that require
the end of life, and those

that go on and on.

Farm Widows, Night Hour

Here come I to cure a burnt sore.
If the dead knew what the living endure,
The burnt sore would burn no more.
—an English charm

If the dead knew
what we the living know,
a lamp might never gutter.

Rather than their usual
extinguishing,
leaving a lash

of wind and smoke,
Godless at last, the dead
might smooth a bedspread,

dampen a forehead,
breathe into our noses
and mouths. *What a chill*

year, we'd wake up saying,
and take another easy
bite, ham watering down

our throats its charming tissue—
full of sun and rain and days
before black blood, when happily

it devoured rotten apple and
apple, alike. Here our old
hands. Difficult hands. We want

a ghost to warm our knuckles,
their swell made by years
of work, years we walked

through half-sleeping, doors
closing softly room after
room behind our bending backs.

Medium on the Dietary Habits of the Dead

What ghosts eat: slippers.
Static. The relative unevenness

of staircases. Migraine aura.
Trump cards. Delicate children.

Smooth flat stones. Fruits candied,
dried, or desiccated. The recently

mated. Zygotes you can pop
like a grape. Bundles of skirt

unmended. Dishcloth carrying
the crumbs and blood

of daily meals. Odd forsakenness.
Metal toys. Rust and Rustoleum.

Soft toys gone mealy under
many a sweaty hand. How much

I miss, my mother. My mother.
Flags ripped apart by wind. The dirt

around the crater where my daughter
was not born.

On Southern Summer Ghosts

Ghosts get hungry in the summer.
You can see them sucking
the sides of jars where

your nieces have captured
lightning bugs, fireflies
that dizzy-throw themselves

against the glass, soft ping
with no echo. Lips glow,
and a ghost gathers what light

it can: the spicket glimmer
of water in the night; dark buttons
in a closet, chipped by a man's

ungentle hands; shoe shine;
every fingernail emerging from
the creek where a girl

sees she isn't young anymore;
where the water travels and we
do not—we roost and rain

sweat under barber poles,
deepen our voices until they crack.

Medium Dreams of Marriage

There were some words
       I promised to have.

Good shoes, good weather.
       Then the whole house

turned upside down into
       the river. Everything

spilled out like a drawer,
       like something that went

unsaid, pans and slippers doing
       their delicate thing

in the water. I was overwhelmed
       by how particulate

the fringe looked hovering over
       my face. The candy jar

again was admirable, dropping
       solidly back

onto its own table. I was a widow
       again so I started snoring

violently, big gulps of water-
       for-air. In my dreams,

there were two trains, crossing
       high up in the air. There were

people on them. One group waved
        to the other, and they slowly

turned and waved to me.
        There was never a husband,

they say. There was never no
        circus. There was no *fair.*

On Being Prolific

A rat can be taught
anything. A rat can

be taught anything,
but this one won't

be taught. I have generously
supplied her with

the bills for the farm,
bills of lading, records

of new geldings. But no
narrative appears. Hard

as a knot, she crouches,
just beyond my hand.

Her hole is filled with words,
but it is not a human

house. It holds a family
small and naked—

I see them born,
then burrowing towards

a nipple to dream pink,
singular dreams—they believe

if you latch on something
hard enough, it will

feed you forever. Outside
the snow is worse

and leaves no light
to write in.

A Dear John Letter

No more numb tongue,
        warrior. No more, young

apostle—no speaking to me
        Sundays. I will sit

on this chair; I will call it
        mine. I will be this hour

a teacher against the light,
        folding piece after

piece of white, papers
        sleeping, dreaming

of the things you put
        on them—lover,

it is under truly relaxing
        stars I have chosen

to give you up. I shake
        extra salt over all

my food. I eat the tidelings,
        sinew and flesh; I take

them as tongues into my belly,
        and they talk. You

are not godless, so you don't
        understand—I have to live

with a little bit of tide
        in my mouth, a little bit

of stamp and turn of heel,
        over and over again;

I have to make
        a slow majesty

out of refrain, the same
        water slapping the same

faults, my old face rising
        in the mirror, most

predictable of moons.
        Go down, satellite.

Go down shrinking and
        quiet and blurred.

Medium on the Sleeping Arrangements
of the Dead

Where the dead sleep: in steel
wool. In sailor's woolen

underwear. Inside timepieces
that will not be wound. Alongside

broken keys. Rat's nests lined
with horoscopes. Silk gloves

too small for a grown daughter's hand.
Chimneys. Old elephant ear plants,

turning yellow and brown creases
against the side of a house. Beneath

a toppled garden angel, wings
pinning her back,

hard into the ground.

Spell for Removals

Soak a tea-bag in blood.
Ask no questions for two days.
Drink nothing that does not

come from your own cupped
hand. File your best knife down
to a sickle sliver. Drain

nothing. The ditches must
sit full and heavy and full
of thought. Kiss your reflection

in the middle of the night.
Cut off your ring; if not possible,
cut off your finger. Bury

both. Or one, then sleep facing
the head of your bed. At your feet
you'll see his eyes, and then

nothing. If you shiver, look
to the north. Don't ever
stop looking.

III.

How to Love a House

God bless the night
creatures. And I

am one, making
my way up and down

the halls, staircase
opening like an accordion,

or flat teeth in a mouth.
This is how you love

a house—be its tongue.
Fleshly pull and press

yourself along its
surfaces. Give off little

wet noises as you
breathe. Stroke down

the banister, and the dust
strokes you back. Soft

skin flakes, fabric,
hair plucked from

a coat, the back
of someone climbing

the upper flights—
the dust is the house.

Love what of you
has been rubbed away.

What of you still
must fall.

Ghost to Apprentice

Doorknobs are easy
to get lost in. Like lakes

for the eye. I love how
your hand goes to them,

again and again. What
are you reaching for?

If we work destiny,
we are bad at it. Adjust

your thinking so it
slants with the roof—

your eyes don't drain
water like eaves.

Throw a leaf around,
if you're desperate.

No one's looking.
Soon you will become

an expert in veins,
rings, the slow music

of a septum when
they're sleeping. Turn over

the pages in a book. That's
what they're expecting.

Something the wind
does. Give them

the next page. What God
doesn't care to do.

The House Says I Love You

Thin slivers of you
embed in me, like glass

in wood—your hair and your
nails. What you wind and

what you cut. I am struck
through with silver

lights, and you wander
like a song, trailing

your chorus. One after
another, your voices go

slack in your throats
like isolated flowers, dark

down to their beginnings.
Sediment is a form

of love—to take on layers,
to compress soot dust

and spider to this fineness—
a grain that marks, that

marks all trespassers—
I feel you, your fingernails

in the wallpaper, curling
it back, evergreen

to black mold sprinkling
silent as the surface

of the moon. Lean into me,
turn a finger-length key—now

revolve, revolve. I won't
give you up.

The Thirst of the Prior Inhabitants

When we were alive, there was a lake.
There was a lake, and it was summer.
The house was already an oddness,

an edifice. And we felt perfectly
inside it, perfectly safe. The gnaws
in the walls were gnaws that were

known, so they were safe. Yet mice
are combatants, much as the ground is.
We talked of damp as something

that rose. We rose and walked many
days to the end of the road, fluttering
coats, and willed the mail to come.

We ignored the moistness in our armpits,
the humid attire of the crotch. We
ignored our mouths, our constant

swallow, the wetness of the forks
on our plates, the end of the meal.
We rose and went to bed. We went

to bed and rose. We glow pink
and soft as roses now. Though
you can barely see us, I suppose.

How winter it is, how quiet. Here
with you, watching you open
your wet little mouth.

Ghost as Housekeeper

I am always waving,
and sometimes clear.

Sometimes in the slick
at the bottom of a frying

pan, a cloud of fat.
All this evening under

the sofa I have lain
untwisting embroidery,

un-plaiting plaids. And
the brown back of it I have

faded to strained tea,
arms polished as a tooth.

Your carelessness
is love to me—as I crease

the newspaper into
its new fallen shape,

a disrupted bird, print
rubbing until the names

are something only
I can read, just as only I

hear the water standing
in the pipes, gallons of it,

pressing—the only sign
the drips, surprisingly

articulate, a Braille
inside the wall.

I wish you could notice
the careful attention

I have given to your
bread—I left you the fairest

flowers, their green marvel
growing on the heel,

pale and dusty.
Like marble, both light

and dark. One antique
spore, and all

can bloom—you say
you cannot eat it,

but I think mold feeds
you more—I want

to give you the silence
of its planet, its heart—

a center which
like mine, is nowhere,

yet increasing.

Ghost in a Dessert Dish

Forgive me. I was never
delicious, only cold.
Now I arrange myself

on a plate in your absence,
staring fish-eyed and jellied
towards the ceiling. There

my heaven is, fissured and clam-
like. I look up as if from
the bottom of a well. I watch you

undress with displeasure—
I wish I could remove
this smoke, this last recollection

of myself—peel it off
like wet stockings.
Even the lips that prefer

whispering. Even my eyelids
that settle, waver like
water spilling over a glass.

Ghost Encounter

From the perspective of a ghost,
we are dull. We are like anything
there in the room, as discrete

as a chair or a lamp—then we move.
The little flicker in the eyes.
That's what gets me, one ghost

says. *Almost like they're*
really alive, like they can see
through the floorboards—not just

a crack of light, but a whole
century, down to dirt, down
a whole cold fathom. Like

they can love something
enough to pass through it—
And they're right. We'll never

know what *curtain* feels,
or *sifter*—blocky as a block
of wood we are, impenetrable,

even our voices—the lowness,
the bright consonants, the thick-
tongued, flat-note sound.

Ghost Trapped in the Attic, Summer Afternoon

So much breath exhaled I can
taste it, shivered out of human

bronchioles. Yellow hot dreams
catch in syrup, drying

linens, the vegetal heat of kudzu
forgetting there ever was

frost; liquid and shaking
is the stream, electric

as an aura, the place
where the sun sits

and traces her way
down the late afternoon.

I can feel the place
where my heart used to be

expanding, really, all
of myself, thick as cotton

against the attic windows,
melting the varnish

on the cradle. Bed posts
blister. The painted flowers

have painful faces, red
and curlicued stamen

extended, mouths hanging
in a gilded frame only

a shade or two off from flame.

Woman in the Diorama

I am in the cold museum
        of your thinking—

now think me a sepia
        thought. Tag

and title me "loved one":
        lay a label on

my fistful of hair. There is
        always the plastic hard

water-curtain. The stage light,
        bugs teeming

under glass. This is nothing

like being afraid. It's carrying
        your leather satchel

into eternity I dislike—it's
        the predictable

marsh extending me this blank
        look. It's the painting

of the cape that never
        comes. And here I am,

kneeling, threading my hook.
        A sea bass opens his mouth

in a silent river, a bottom lip
         collecting another, then

another white piece of dust.

Suicide Ghost

Death is not a precise activity.
Just aim in the general

direction. Then *there*,
you've got it. Got what?

Nothing. That's about right.
Almost right. It's almost right

and straight on until
morning, though nothing

is thereafter straight. I have
a vision now of one of those

cats that mummified,
stuck behind the pipe organ,

going for that one eternal
mouse. No one thinks

they're going to become
a stray leather purse, an easily

mistakable grocery bag,
damp and flattened

in the outer lots where,
I have heard it said,

the women circle.
We want to call everything

planetary, but really
there's much more cosmic

dust—debris, you could say.
But that implies that there

was something there before,
something whole, now blown

apart—very often I held a piece
of glass in my hand,

and licked it, started
to curl my flesh

around it, just to the point
of blood. I do not know,

I never did, what the hell any
human heart was ever doing.

Hunter

I'll open no other—
        a tree-lined soul is mine—

I'm not a ground
        that you can cover, harbor

green, leaf green. The hard return
        of my Winchester hurts me.

I feel its dark body
        on my arms, talk-talking

to me. Hum of index, my finger
        slipping to its stock—

I want to say something about
        light here, I want to say

something like a name. I want
        to imagine you here,

wet and open, wind and wave.
        Shaking your terrible hands.

You move right through me.
        And the black plums

of my feet are sweetly bled.
        Dire horse, dire man.

I fled you, and then you fled.

Ghost Coming to Terms

It is highly likely
that I am dead or,

at least, differently
alive. There are stories

I keep telling myself—
I left my face in an ashtray

at a party; I folded up
my genitals and mailed

them in the wrong card,
wrong address, not

returned to sender. It is
possible I am a very bad

kind of fruit. It is possible
that the anatomy dummy

I was once handed has
now been disassembled.

Thieves. Who took him
from me? I open cabinet

after cabinet, convinced
I'll find an organ

I can call my own. *Here,*
Kidney, Kidney.

A cat answers, *Now-now,*
but that's not exactly

the same. From dust and sand
on the floor, I look up

at the picture window, the face
of Jesus, saying: *Brevity,*

brevity. And it doesn't
hurt me at all.

That's how I know.

The Anniversary Dream

Sometimes, you fall in love
       with the man who killed you.

You want to be close
       to him. You want to feel

and fondle his ears. They are
       slow divers, floating

down the hill in dusk. They are
       coins going to the bottom

of an ocean. They were coins
       you wanted to spend.

After the Butchering

One of my hearts is dead.
The other is in the backyard,

sleeping under a stone.
I buried it in a piece of wool

I decided had to go away.
One of my hands is intelligent—

it speaks to the other, who responds
only in low monotones, the trance

of strength without skill. All evening
I watched a man batter a tree

with a blade. If you are going to kill,
you have to be good at it, my right hand

says to the other. My left hand hums
to the pot handle, the whispering meat

on the stove, sending up clouds
I won't hesitate to call heaven.

A Shadow Left My Party

A Shadow left my party
and started climbing stairs—

did not stop at any landing,
stepped quietly, laid itself

down at the foot of my bed
like a pair of stockings,

and it waits for me with
a serious kind of closeness

like when someone leans
into your ear to whisper

of some senior so-and-so's
misfortune, a blood vessel's backfire,

reminding me of the brains
in all our skulls, wet and silent

like the walnuts outside
my window in the rain.

The distortion of the glass,
catching my face just there—

shaded, disappointed,
eyebrows smudging together like

a horizon line, hillside
waiting for the snow.

Acknowledgments

Many thanks to the editors of the following publications in which these poems previously appeared, sometimes in different forms:

The Adroit Journal: "Ghost as Housekeeper"

Anti-: "Medium Dreams of Marriage"

Black Warrior Review: "After the Butchering"

Boulevard: "Ghost Encounter"

Chattahoochee Review: "To the Salt Gator"

Court Green: "Medium in the Morning," "Medium on the Dietary Habits of the Dead," "Suicide Ghost"

Fiolet and Wing: An Anthology of Domestic Fabulism: "The Thirst of the Prior Inhabitants"

Gingerbread House Literary Magazine: "Witch as Healer"

Glass: A Journal of Poetry: "Medium after Producing the Ectoplasm," "A Shadow Left My Party"

Harpur Palate: "Dream of Flat Hills"

High Chair: "The Anniversary Dream," "A Dear John Letter"

Indiana Review: "Ghost to Apprentice"

The Marriage, a chapbook from Horse Less Press: "Witch in Winter," "Witch to Familiar"

Matter: A Journal of Political Poetry and Commentary: "Collector of Luck," "Spell for a Daughter"

Midwestern Gothic: "Where to Look for Ghosts"

Nashville Review: "Woman in the Diorama"

Phantom Drift: A Journal of New Fabulism: "The House Says I Love You," "Witch as La Belle Dame"

Radar Poetry: "Personal Cleansings," "Spell for a Lover," "Witch Doctrine: On Giving Prescriptions," "Witch Dreams of Happiness," "Witch Questions the So-Called Higher Power"

Requited Journal: "Witch Doctrine: Comfort" and "Witch Lullaby"

RHINO Poetry: "Southern Witch Doctrine on the Resurrection"

Southern Indiana Review: "Ghost in a Dessert Dish"

Transom: "Hunter"

Third Coast: "Farm Widows, Night Hour"

Willow Springs: "Dear Ghost:," "Final Witch Doctrine"

*

I wish to thank the other creative and scholarly minds whose support helped me write this book: my doctoral committee, Christina Pugh, Roger Reeves, Mark Canuel, Jennifer Ashton, and Tony Trigilio; my MFA thesis committee, Carl Philips, Mary Jo Bang, and Kerri Webster; Carol Ann Davis, who started me on this journey many years ago at the College of Charleston; my colleagues at the University of Illinois-Chicago and Washington University in St. Louis; Vermont Studio Center, which gave me a magical month of residency to finish these poems; the writers and friends who read these poems and many others as they grew and changed over the years: Alec Hershman, Brooke Wonders, Philip Matthews, Brianna Noll, Virginia Konchan, Katya Kulik, and Sacha Siskonen; and Kate Everitt, who was there from the beginning.

For their exquisite care in bringing this book into the world, I extend much gratitude to the University of Akron Press team, especially to Jon Miller, Amy Freels, and Mary Biddinger. Thank you, Amy, for making this book so physically beautiful, and thank you, Mary, for everything. Your dedication to poetry and your kindness inspire me.

I also thank my family, most of all my parents, Janis and Bill Browning: there are not enough words in the world to say how grateful I am for your unfailing love and support. Thank you for believing in me.

This book is dedicated to the women in my family, past and present. Janis Browning, Willie Mae "Tip" Frazier Browning, and Jennie V. Jones Crow: this is for you.

Annah Browning is the author of a chapbook, *The Marriage* (Horse Less Press, 2013) and poetry editor and cofounder of *Grimoire Magazine*. Her poetry has appeared in *Indiana Review, Black Warrior Review, Willow Springs, Boulevard,* and elsewhere. She earned her MFA from Washington University in St. Louis and her PhD from the University of Illinois at Chicago. Originally from the foothills of South Carolina, she now calls Chicago home.

Printed in the United States
By Bookmasters